E♭ BARITONE SAXOPHONE

MOVIE FAVORITES

Solos and Band Arrangements
Correlated with Essential Elements Band Method

Arranged by
MICHAEL SWEENEY

Welcome to Essential Elements Movie Favorites! There are two versions of each selection in this versatile book. The SOLO version appears on the left-hand page of your book. The FULL BAND arrangement appears on the right-hand page. Optional accompaniment recordings are available separately in CD or cassette format. Use these recordings when playing solos for friends and family.

Solo Pg.	Band Arr. Pg.	Title	Correlated with Essential Elements
2	3	Theme from "Jurassic Park"	Book 1, page 19
4	5	Chariots Of Fire	Book 1, page 19
6	7	The Man From Snowy River	Book 1, page 19
8	9	Forrest Gump – Main Title (Feather Theme)	Book 1, page 29
10	11	Somewhere Out There	Book 1, page 29
12	13	The John Dunbar Theme	Book 1, page 29
14	15	Raiders March	Book 2, page 14
16	17	Apollo 13 (End Credits)	Book 2, page 14
18	19	Theme From E.T. (The Extra-Terrestrial)	Book 2, page 14
20	21	Star Trek® - The Motion Picture	Book 2, page 29
22	23	Back To The Future	Book 2, page 29

ISBN 978-0-7935-5968-8

HAL•LEONARD™
CORPORATION
7777 W. BLUEMOUND RD. P.O. BOX 13819 MILWAUKEE, WI 53213

00860024

FROM The Universal Motion Picture JURASSIC PARK

Theme From "JURASSIC PARK"

E♭ BARITONE SAXOPHONE
Solo

Composed by JOHN WILLIAMS
Arranged by MICHAEL SWEENEY

MCA music publishing

Theme From "JURASSIC PARK"

Eb BARITONE SAXOPHONE
Band Arrangement

Composed by JOHN WILLIAMS
Arranged by MICHAEL SWEENEY

MCA music publishing

From CHARIOTS OF FIRE

CHARIOTS OF FIRE

E♭ BARITONE SAXOPHONE
Solo

Music by VANGELIS
Arranged by MICHAEL SWEENEY

00860024

CHARIOTS OF FIRE

Eb BARITONE SAXOPHONE
Band Arrangement

Music by VANGELIS
Arranged by MICHAEL SWEENEY

00860024

From THE MAN FROM SNOWY RIVER

THE MAN FROM SNOWY RIVER
(Main Title Theme)

Eb BARITONE SAXOPHONE
Solo

By BRUCE ROWLAND
Arranged by MICHAEL SWEENEY

00860024

THE MAN FROM SNOWY RIVER
(Main Title Theme)

Eb BARITONE SAXOPHONE
Band Arrangement

By BRUCE ROWLAND
Arranged by MICHAEL SWEENEY

00860024

From The Paramount Motion Picture FORREST GUMP
FORREST GUMP - MAIN TITLE
(Feather Theme)

E♭ **BARITONE SAXOPHONE**
Solo

Music by ALAN SILVESTRI
Arranged by MICHAEL SWEENEY

From The Paramount Motion Picture FORREST GUMP

FORREST GUMP - MAIN TITLE
(Feather Theme)

E♭ BARITONE SAXOPHONE
Band Arrangement

Music by ALAN SILVESTRI
Arranged by MICHAEL SWEENEY

00860024

From AN AMERICAN TAIL
Somewhere Out There

Words and Music by JAMES HORNER,
BARRY MANN and CYNTHIA WEIL
Arranged by MICHAEL SWEENEY

E♭ BARITONE SAXOPHONE
Solo

MCA music publishing

From AN AMERICAN TAIL

SOMEWHERE OUT THERE

Words and Music by JAMES HORNER,
BARRY MANN and CYNTHIA WEIL
Arranged by MICHAEL SWEENEY

Eb BARITONE SAXOPHONE
Band Arrangement

MCA music publishing

From DANCES WITH WOLVES

THE JOHN DUNBAR THEME

Eb BARITONE SAXOPHONE
Solo

By John Barry
Arranged by MICHAEL SWEENEY

00860024

From **DANCES WITH WOLVES**
THE JOHN DUNBAR THEME

E♭ BARITONE SAXOPHONE
Band Arrangement

By JOHN BARRY
Arranged by MICHAEL SWEENEY

00860024

From The Paramount Motion Picture RAIDERS OF THE LOST ARK

RAIDERS MARCH

Eb BARITONE SAXOPHONE
Solo

By JOHN WILLIAMS
Arranged by MICHAEL SWEENEY

RAIDERS MARCH

Eb **BARITONE SAXOPHONE**
Band Arrangement

By JOHN WILLIAMS
Arranged by MICHAEL SWEENEY

00860024

From APOLLO 13
APOLLO 13
(End Credits)

E♭ BARITONE SAXOPHONE
Solo

By JAMES HORNER
Arranged by MICHAEL SWEENEY

MCA music publishing

From APOLLO 13
APOLLO 13
(End Credits)

E♭ BARITONE SAXOPHONE
Band Arrangement

By JAMES HORNER
Arranged by MICHAEL SWEENEY

MCA music publishing

00860024

From The Universal Picture E.T. (THE EXTRA-TERRESTRIAL)

THEME FROM E.T. (THE EXTRA-TERRESTRIAL)

E♭ BARITONE SAXOPHONE
Solo

Music by JOHN WILLIAMS
Arranged by MICHAEL SWEENEY

MCA music publishing

THEME FROM E.T. (THE EXTRA-TERRESTRIAL)

B♭ BARITONE SAXOPHONE
Band Arrangement

Music by JOHN WILLIAMS
Arranged by MICHAEL SWEENEY

MCA music publishing

Theme From The Paramount Picture STAR TREK
STAR TREK®-THE MOTION PICTURE

E♭ BARITONE SAXOPHONE
Solo

Music by JERRY GOLDSMITH
Arranged by MICHAEL SWEENEY

STAR TREK®-THE-MOTION PICTURE

E♭ BARITONE SAXOPHONE
Band Arrangement

Music by JERRY GOLDSMITH
Arranged by MICHAEL SWEENEY

00860024

From The Universal Motion Picture BACK TO THE FUTURE

BACK TO THE FUTURE

E♭ BARITONE SAXOPHONE
Solo

By ALAN SILVESTRI
Arranged by MICHAEL SWEENEY

MCA music publishing

BACK TO THE FUTURE

Eb BARITONE SAXOPHONE
Band Arrangement

By ALAN SILVESTRI
Arranged by MICHAEL SWEENEY

MCA music publishing